Mass for the Grace of a Happy Death

Frank X. Gaspar

1994 Anhinga Prize for Poetry

Joy Harjo, Judge

Tallahassee, Florida

1994

Library of Congress Cataloging in Publication Data

Gaspar, Frank X.
Mass for the Grace of a Happy Death

(The Anhinga Prize for Poetry, 1994)
I. Title II. Series: Anhinga Poetry Prize Series
Library of Congress Catalog Card Number 94-073736
ISBN: 0-938078-38-0

Printed in the United States of America
First Edition: February 1995

Cover Art and Design by David Wilder
Editing and Production by Rex West and Rick Campbell

Anhinga Press thanks the following people for their help in
selecting this manuscript from nearly 600 entries: Devan Cook, Pat
MacEnulty, Kitty Gretsch, Debra Pallone Parks, Mary Jane Ryals,
Michael Trammell, Tom Heise, Douglas Ford, Darrel Fike, Frances
Brock, Toni Whitfield, Andrea Kelly, Karen Janowsky, Kevin Casey,
Dan Damerville, Susan Damerville, Clare Raulerson, Sharon
Weightman, Sandra Teichmann, Nancy Applegate, Genevieve
Fager, Helen Wallace, Vicki Hunt, and Thom Chesney.

Anhinga Press, Inc. is a nonprofit corporation staffed largely by
volunteers dedicated wholly to the publication and appreciation of
fine poetry. Director: Rick Campbell. Board of Directors: Van K.
Brock, Donna Long, Lynne Knight, Stephanie Sgouros, Joann
Gardner, Melanie Rawls, Geoffrey Brock, Martina Schmid, and
Rex West.

Publication of this book is sponsored in part by the Florida
Department of State, Division of Cultural Affairs, and the Florida
Arts Council.

Anhinga Press. PO Box 10595. Tallahassee, FL 32302. USA

0= 33 8 2 7 63 4

Acknowledgments

Poems in this book originally appeared in the following magazines:

The Antioch Review ("Chronicle") • *The Denver Quarterly* ("Boston") • *Faultline* ("Mexican Woman, Hair in Braids, Caught in Barbed Wire on the Side of I-5" and "Love is the Power Which Impels One to Seek the Beautiful") • *The Georgia Review* ("Underwood" and "Coal") • *The Gettysburg Review* ("Mission," "What Death with Love Must Have to Do," and "The Wine at Cana") • *The Hudson Review* ("Lamentation," "Winter Berries," and "Eucharist") • *The James River Review* ("My Aunt Among the Lilies," "Christ in the World of Matter," and "Sand") • *Kenyon Review* ("Where Do You Sleep?") • *The Massachusetts Review* ("Work") • *The Nation* ("Lookouts, Foul Weather") • *The New England Review* ("Gall, Wormwood," and "Old Stories") • *Nimrod* ("Crows," and "Psalm") • *Pearl* ("South") • *Prairie Schooner* ("Angels" and "Walking Out in Fog") • *Provincetown Arts* ("Codeine," and "Mass for the Grace of a Happy Death") • *Sewanee Review* ("Beggars and Angels" and "Hymn") • *Tampa Review* ("Absolution," and "Stealing") • *Western Humanities Review* ("R and R") • *WigWag* ("At Sea, Tonkin").

"Where Do You Sleep?" has been reprinted in the anthology *Cultural Tapestry*, HarperCollins, 1991.

"South" and "Curandera" have been reprinted in the anthology *Grand Passion: The Poets of Los Angeles and Beyond*, Red Winds Books, 1995.

The author wishes to thank the National Endowment for the Arts for a grant which aided in the completion of this book. Special thanks to Allen Bundy, Stephen Perry, and Diann Blakely Shoaf.

For Georgia, for John, and for the Old Ones.

Mass for the Grace of a Happy Death

I. CHRONICLE

II. LAMENTATION

III. PSALM

Notes

*The Mass is a true sacrifice with propitiatory and
supplicatory value.*

— *Council of Trent, 1562*

*In the Mass each person has an office to perform; the
people take part by means of acclamations, responses,
psalmody, antiphons, and songs, as well as by actions,
gestures, bodily attitudes, and a reverent silence at the
proper time.*

— *The Saint Joseph Catechism*

> *And prayer is more
> Than an order of words, the conscious occupation
> Of the praying mind, or the sound of the voice praying.
> And what the dead had no speech for, when living,
> They can tell you, being dead: the communication
> Of the dead is tongued with fire beyond the language
> of the living.*

— *Little Gidding*

I.
CHRONICLE

—They are all gone into the world of light

Old Stories

They would gather around the table
and pull down the whiskey and the small glasses,
their arms and chests still thick as barrels
under their baggy shirts and sweaters,
though their walking was stooped, their big hands
stiff-fisted and unsteady, their hair gone white
or gray as though it had taken on the colors
of the winter ocean that they loved to tell about,
going back to the time when they patrolled as surfmen
along the beaches—the old Coast Guard's Lifesavers.
My great uncle always drank off his first shot quickly
then poured himself another and let it stand
and stared into it, telling it what the waves
looked like, not a gleam of light in them, like stone
he'd say, like unfaced stone the size of hills
pounding at you, and in those gales the blowing snow
would smother any lights ashore, and the barges
and barques and schooners, blind and crossripped,
would ground themselves on the miles of bars,
and the sea would beat them back to timber.
If dawn ever came for those sailors, they'd see
the shore looming, a line of ice
and surf in white thunder, the Coast Guard
in ready position on the frozen beach
with their Lyle Guns and horse carts, waiting grimly
for a chance to shoot a line out or launch
a surfboat into the breaking swell. This
is how the stories would go, passing back
and forth among those old, old men, always coming
around to courage and strength and death,
and mostly to death, the splintered boat, the twist
in the line, the falling spar, the cold, and each
man had his claim to having beaten it once or more,
and he'd tell you about everything, about the itch
of cold sweat under wool, about breath freezing

to rime-frost on a mustache, about the rant
of ocean that made a man's shout so small and useless.
You can still see the bars today, creamy
under the blue surf, the good sand beach
curving to the sea the way it has since the glacier.
Behind you the dunes roll away to the sky,
and in winter there's still the wind to teach you humility.
Sometimes yet in a big blow, the old soft bones
of some dead vessel groan up from sand and water
where they have lain for a hundred years,
rising now from burial as if to claim
their vanished flesh in this new cold light.
Sometimes my great-uncle would pull me to his side
and hold me there, his voice already sounding
as though it came from another room, and he'd work
his way over the dunes along his patrol, night,
gale-winds, close by the booming of those killing breakers,
and I'd feel his hand ticking slow time
on my shoulders, hear him saying, *This is for you—
Remember this*.... And I'd feel him slacken
just the way the weather sags when a hard rain is over,
a tired body exhaling and settling
after a quick pounding of the heart.

Gall, Wormwood

We'd lie under wasting stones at night
in the old cemetery and toke the rum
and cheap wine that we always wheedled
some Summer Person into buying for us
because we were Townies and under age.
Down along the honky-tonk waterfront we knew

the town swelled in its nightly raptures,
the meat-rack hustle, the tourist bars,
the easy tricks, night-laughs that always
carried to our ears from some other world
so rich and evil we could only desire it.
We improvised on the dust of our ancient dead

whose stones had sugared away their names,
one set of graves like a circle of toadstools,
a young wife, we decided, six of her children.
Elsewhere leaned markers on empty loam, shadows
of words under lichen—*In Memoriam, Lost at Sea.*
We waited, drunk, for their ghosts to claim us,

dared and mocked them—and they never came.
They lay in the deeps of oblivion and grinned
at nothing until we stumbled down the soft hill
stretching toward the town's late music,
some reek of theirs trailing behind us
as we roamed among the husks of the living.

Work

To lift the flesh
from the fine sheer bone
so the fish's body fell
back into an image of fish,
head and fin joined
in a wicked mockery
of wholeness—that
was one genius of his hands
that never left with age
or gout or whiskey, and one
measure of a man he passed
to me, leaving me his black knife
which he'd honed to a rib
on oil and stone and showing
me the lines of the body
one follows, drawing the blade
like a feather over skin,
lifting the pearl of binding scales
and opening the shining harvest
of fish, meat for one hunger
and for another: in the sweat
of his face, his right to travel
in that vanishing, uncomplicated
world of men where he bid me
to follow with grace and anger,
showed me the proper silence
of labor, how to hold my mouth
shut with the exact insurgent
tuck of lip, how he wanted me
to glare back, as he did, into
the hard light of abundance
and tear the bread from any
long task we had set before us.

Chronicle

—Old Man Coelho, Years Back, at the V.F.W. Bar

We slipped our lines with the tide,
never a moon, stifled the croak
of the oars with rags and ran
down the wind until it was safe
to hoist sail. From there we knew
we would need to beat back to windward,
make for the harbor's mouth and slip
to open sea. Three of us then, your ma's
old man, Tony D. and myself, and I
was just a kid then, stupid. We knew
those sharpies from New Bedford
would be hove-to in the swells
off the narrow bars—we'd done it before,
seen them up on the big decks with their pistols—
and they scared us, believe it. But it always
went off without a hitch. They'd lower
the hootch in a cargo net, and your ma's old man
would send up the money in a lobster basket,
and we'd close-haul to windward home, catch the tide.
All this before dawn. That one time
we knew something was wrong, though,
saw the black shadows of cars parked next
to Tony D.'s fish truck down at Fiddler's wharf,
and Tony D. says "Let me ashore down to East'd."
I thought for a minute he'd lost his balls,
but your ma's old man said, "Let him go."
And then Tony says, "After you leave me off
you take down the sail and drift awhile."
We sat in the slough about a mile out
and pretty soon we hear the sirens,
and we look and there's the whole end
of the Atlantic Fisheries wharf going
up afire. We knew what to do then.

We come back in to the Fiddler's Wharf
while every man and boy in town was down
to Atlantic Fisheries. Tony D. met us
and we loaded up his old truck just
like we'd planned, and drove her right
up the Cape and did our business. "Tony,"
I said, "What the hell did you do?" He
never said a word. Never. Nothing.
That was the last trip your grandfather made,
and me, too. Tony kept after it, though.
That's how he got the money for
The *Coracao de Jesus*, his first trawler.
I never went on the water with him after that—
afraid of him, I suppose, though he
was a good captain by all accounts.
And you know all about how he went
back to old country finally, where he died
happy, a big house with servants,
a grave in the old soil near where he was born.
I'm worn out and good for nothing now—you can't
imagine me doing those things, nor Tony D., nor
your grandfather, dead all this time.
I did though, and I'm glad of it, too.
A lot of men lost their jobs from that fire—
those were hard times, and they never
built the wharf back—but
it doesn't seem like anything
to me now. It's like nothing in the world.
I'd do it again, too, just for
the feel of it when that wharf
went up, but I didn't know that
about me then. I didn't know
that Tony D. was the only one
among us had any sense at all.

My Aunt Among the Lilies

There were never lilies.
Irises grew in a bricked
row along the front of the house,
hollyhocks spined up behind
our hedge, and morning glories
bruised the fence
with their bitter mouths.
I could watch her, the light
swelling from the flowers
and catching in the hollows
of her throat, deepening
the hazel shine of her skin
as though some deed of youth
had been passed to her, some
covenant of renewal. But then
some long-remembered shade
would cross her face. Why
did she ever walk this way,
along the strict borders
of the house, her dress
puckered in the summer heat,
her Rosary laced at her wrist?
For hers was not an earthly
mission—no concern for
the watering can or rake
or spade. I saw her reach
once into a corner of moss
and bring out a cricket
perched on the curl
of her arthritic hand, watch
it with wonder and then
drop it, crush it
beneath the stub of her
black heel. She rose
then on heavy breath
and loomed over the yard
like some dark saint come
to harrow this world
of violent conversions.

The Abandoned Dump

Which everyone who could remember
called simply The Old Dump, a pale
depression in the cluttered pines
at the end of a soft sand road, gone
unused for at least a generation, place
where you might go with a clamrake to dig
gently for fancy bottles to boil and set
on the sill of a sun-facing window, something
the woman did that day in fall, pulling
her gentle dog along behind her, lavishing
her heart and independence on the woods
so ripe with pine and the shush of wind
in the fragrant boughs. It was her own
idea to turn a few spadefuls of black
earth before searching, taking the level
down a few more years by her reckoning,
thinking back upon the story she had read
about the man who searched for Troy because
he fell so much in love with Homer that he
had no recourse but to believe; and found
the city and others beneath it, convinced
himself he'd found the tomb of Priam when
his shovels reached a cache of gold.
                    So when her own shovel
touched something and she eased the rake
until that skull rolled up like a dumb melon
she was not fooled into thinking she had found
something remarkable. I don't believe she
could have spun more than one or two wild tales
in her head in the short moment when her breath
uncaught and everything tightened along her
arms and shoulders and she looked around at
the cool woods and continued raking, pulling up
the rest, scattered, cluttered, femurs, patellas,
the feet and hands like cropped dice, pieces

she would never piece together, as we would
never piece together exactly what it was
passed through her mind as she wrapped
that plunder in her barn-coat and lugged
it off like an old woodgatherer, laying
it out on the wine-dark rug in her parlor
where she worked over it all winter, failing
ultimately to get each piece to fit, and
by her own accounts going back and raking
more to see if other bones might still be
buried, caked in the wet, hard dirt. The
Selectmen searched the rolls as far back
as they went, and no name could be hung
about the man (it *was* a man, this from
the county doctor who was summoned in
after the boy told what he'd seen through
the tripped door one Sunday). Why she
refused and then had to be forced to let
it go is what everyone talks about in all
the muttered versions: One simply
could say *lonely* or *crazy*, but no one
knew her that way. You could pity her,
thinking she might not have figured
the dangers, but how many here in the town
have ever taken their passion as far, have been
that willing to suffer for it?
                                And the talk
always goes back to those anonymous bones
moldering in the trash, someone who walked
among us and fell into oblivion and was
resurrected, brought into the light, and loved.

Winter Berries

Now it is Christmas in the woods
and the pines are hung with gloomy light,
the black silk on the pond's eye
has clouded in its wax of ice,
and two boys that I remember
have come to gather red berries
and the boughs of the white pine,
an idea that no one put them up to
although they talk about their mothers
as though such a thing might make
a happiness around the doors of a house,
as though only the women would know
what to do with an armload of red and green:
And it's my friend and I walking
the corrupt ice of the pond until
we see the purple tangle of the winterberry bush
and the yellow stalks of the dead reeds
and suddenly his legs burst through
in a great crash and gush—up to his knees
in the shallow water, and he curses
and lumbers to shore, smashing a wake
of splintered ice while I, a few feet away
walk as though charmed. Later, sacks filled
with berries and on a dark hill hacking
the bottommost tender branches of pine,
we see that his brown pants have frozen
and he bends them, makes them crackle
around the instep of his boot. I don't
have to ask if he is cold. His face is
flushed and young and beautiful,
though I would not have said so then,
but now, refracted across so much memory and longing
it darkens any recollection that might follow it:
I know we must have hiked home in the short
winter dusk with our arms full of garland,

but I don't recall our mothers' greetings
nor can I remember the sprays on the weathered doors
or windowsills, nor the Christmas lights
of that particular year. And the boys,
who have gone forward into the brambles
of what we call *lives*, are gone forever
except for the persistent traces in one
mind or another, never to be trusted, already
passed into the intricate fiction of what is behind.
Longing for what, then? When the sun
draws behind the low hills west of the pond,
the alder still purples, the winter-dead
grasses still bleach in the bone cold: even
though new houses break the clean lines
of thicket, there is a luster that comes up
in moments before the sky gives over
to the waiting stars: no matter how you watch it,
you cannot gauge the precise moment it vanishes,
you cannot be sure what you wanted to rush to
and gather in your arms and save.

Walking Out in Fog

Like the surprised angels in Chagall's
rare world, or those dreamy mosaics
of the Divine Constantine, your feet
would scarcely touch a black paving-stone
if you walked out with me:
You'd float as I believe
I sometimes do under the wet eaves
of the darkened houses,
down the long halls of the dead elms,
on the last breath of the foghorns,
coming finally
to the town's watery end
where we can do nothing
but turn back again
or stand dumb in the false light, tempted
once more by the old idea that the sea
might stand for something radiant beyond our senses,
or that this land's end might be
a pallid emblem—that our lives
really *are* small things, and must be touched
gently or be torn beyond restoring,
like a spotted moth's wing I crushed once
as a child, meaning no harm,
meaning only a kind of homage
to what I know now
is that quality Goethe described,
saying that in everything transitory
is a metaphor for the unknowable.
In this hush, nothing passes.
I can hear a dory chafe
its painter's splice against
a mooring ring, and just
as easily I can judge
how each footfall

that ever raised a summer's dust here
has filed its way among
the mute forms of the vanished trees.
And when you hear the lone
clear note of the struck bell
rising from its buoy,
you will think it prospers
like a strange kind of love,
for we can think of nothing else
to call it, even while it flies to us
over the water, even as it becomes
itself again, clanging its warning,
falling silent.

Absolution

At night the old houses lean together
like a clan gathered to gossip at
the lip of a common well: shingles
soften under the long stains of moss,
and a cold dew crawls down the reflective
panes of the windows. This is not your town
but another, wholly mine, a place
of the beatified dead, part Hopper painting
part old story, white pickets and primroses,
and yards and streets of sand as pale
as the meal of crushed bone. No one
ever shows a face, but the geraniums
are clearly tended, the porch-swings
groomed and maintained. The ghosts
here are charged in the eternal happiness
of bad art: there is not a ruptured
kidney in the place, no bad tooth, no
bloody cough, and the sea is bountiful
and terrible, and even the children's
polished graves are serene and proper
under their white hills of sand. I entered
a house once, a cottage with oil lamps
and tulle curtains breathing in the open
doorway. I came to steal brass and touch
the old papers in the hollow desk. I walked
through the small, tidy rooms, thinking
that I could still be saved. Surely
one of the invisible would come forth
and lay a wafer on my tongue, transfigure
me into everything I should have been,
raise me to abstraction: beauty, goodness.
But every dream ends badly. We come back.
When we roll our legs over to the floor,
pad to the kitchen for our morning coffee,
what presence can we imagine vanishing
through the shaved walls and slatted blinds,
absolving us to return to this body?

Christ in the World of Matter

Consider His head, bloody, lolled
to one side, His side bloody too,
the spear's wound painted as a careful slit
giving forth, as in the scripture,
water also, and His carved body—shadows
from the votive candles fluttering over it,
the light washing Him in the pale
gray-green of death, His feet pierced
by a single nail, the trail of blood
gleaming there in a squib of polish, and when
we looked up at Him from the communion rail
it was never into His eyes, for He looked away,
some genius in the artisan's touch
having drawn His gaze to an inner distance,
flattened, hollow and beyond reach,
not the face of God here, not the one
passed down to us from *Exodus, Kings,
Daniel, Mark, Revelations*—all the fires
gone dead, all the passions blanched, all
except those of the anonymous maker,
someone who graved the appetites of creation
in the broken curve of the body,
the crown of utter ruin.

Reliquary

Bone of the manatee
and the carved yellow tooth
of the sperm whale, the number
of barrels of oil tried from its fat
penciled next to the old name
in the tooth's hollow — whale killed
in 1912 by my great uncle,
this from memory, for the relics
have been bargained away from our door
by the traveling antique dealers,
my mother remembering the hard times
of some previous winter and letting
everything go for a thin rick of dollars:
brass compass boxed in mahogany, harpoon's
lily, case-knife, the blue serge uniform,
even the coffin flag, for little goes down
to the lockers of death with the body as once
it did, the daggers of the old sailors
laid by their sides in the burial boats,
the boats laid under the rich bogs
to fester in the holy nitrogen
where nothing followed and no one
came after, and above, on the crown
of the earth, the mourner's foot
stepping quietly to a song. *Mother,*
what winter was it that stripped us
of all the implements of that life?
I remember snow moaning up the ditch
from the harbor and fog on our breath
in the bedrooms. Now I must
remember everything. *Where is our bone?*
Where has that scored tooth gone?

Acts

As if there were no bitterness
in their lives, as if no dark ever
slid outward from the sills of
those kiltered windows, the house
would suddenly fill with women
and the rooms would float in heady
yeasts while my mother, powdered
to the wrists in flour, would pound
the dough in the great bowl, yellow,
sugared, egg-heavy, warm in the gossip
and coal-smoke of a winter morning.
And the gravid bowl set by the chimney
filled each corner with lingering
spirits, the sweet bread swelling,
buttock, breast, belly, plump tub
of the world where the women even then
were softly disappearing into their
envies and wishes, and where the men
also slipped toward shadows as they waited
for the hot slabs tendered from the oven,
greased with butter, to dredge
in milked coffee after a freezing day
at the wharves: and the oldest
among them all, maple-skinned, gaunt
under her rough apron, brushing
the heel of her hand in the Sign
of the Cross over still-rising loaves,
a devotion she would never again
make over loaves like these,
never again in exactly this way,
the earth, in the rife bounty
it heaps upon the favored, letting
go of all of this forever: If such
sweet bread were ever blessed or holy,
let them take it now, quickly—and eat.

Beggars and Angels

That day the angel came and stiffened
the clothes that hung on the weeping lines
between the house and the woodshed,
and the world turned white as a wing
under the shining edict of frost:
Take them in, my mother said,
as if beggars had come to the door,
and we shuffled out in the embroidered cold,
basket between us, gloves off for picking
the live wooden pins from their freight,
collecting the workpants, my brother's
green shirts, the sheets and towels
that would not let go of their last ecstatic
postures, crunching as we forced them
into the narrow wicker, and some we
simply laid like planks, our fingers numbing
in the stippled air as we pulled and culled,
sometimes our shoulders and hands touching,
my mother looking old by the gray at her face
but deft at her work, collecting the empty
forms of the body, and then back into
the house where we sat at the table
with tea and milk and the time passing
and those transfigured shapes sighing
in the steady heat of the stoves.

Coal

We woke to the sound of anthracite
sliding down the truck's long chute
and ran to the window to see snow
spitting over the heaved walk
and the men hauling the big hods into the shed
with their perfect balance, their leaning shoulders
and jutting hips, quick-stepping, someplace
else to get to, the morning going off
to that fossil midden of days
where we come now to rake and sift,
as we did then in the dark bins
when no one thought to look for us,
when we could disappear among the black sooty
paragons of coal—this in the time before art
and language, with only God making us promises,
spreading His truth in the aromatics of kerosene
and the iron rust of axeheads and saws,
in coal dust in slow galactic drift before
the plain field of the shed window, in absolute
equations of time and matter coming down
around our ears and filling our noses and heaping
their bounty upon eyelash and hay-rake.
Our quick hearts beat at the edge of winter,
and a sudden voice called out, sharp as air,
and the moment receded according to all
the scriptures of nature, once, once,
and the small, pale-knuckled hands rummaged,
rubbing the chinked facets of coal, bringing out
the feathery traces of the long-dead ferns and leaves,
those dim ghosts polished, locked in falling light.

Underwood

Once in summer light
he turned to me and said
When you die, you die —
that's it. There's not
anything else. This parses
like a dream, but it is not.
He worked on a neighbor's wall,
a pail of whitewash by his shoes.
Sallow weeds bowed and yawned,
and I had no business listening
to this blasphemous talk coming
from an old-country Catholic.
Another time he came up the walk
with an old black Underwood portable
that the failed restaurant
on the corner had used
for typing its sandwich menus.
A gift for me. Five dollars.
It smelled like oil and steel
and clattered back at the world
when we poked it. This
would be another act of love
that made me. Now what
do I say about this grave
in the clumped thicket
of lilac and alder,
on the Church's scruffy hillside
where the wind sloughs
and tatters to ribbons
against the quick branches,
the simple stone?

Crows

One of the great February storms,
bales of snow packed along the yards
and roads, and the woods waist-deep
where we waded and wallowed in the old
men's boots, carefully skirted
the blanked ponds and dragged
our duffels to the hut we had made
all summer and fall, where we'd wedged
the crate-wood roof over the split pine
beams and thatched it with needles
and cadged a stove from the dump
and hinges for the door. Night
we huddled in sleeping bags, burned
green wood, slept toward dawn
and woke early, the world white
and silent, cracked a fire
and cooked eggs, loaded our rifles,
and high in the pines the crows
grew heedful, their bodies smoldering
and the sky squalling in their yellow throats,
God, God, God, shaking the wet powder
from the uppermost trees when they sprang
into the sober air and dipped and rose
and settled beyond the close hills,
still calling their noise to one another,
to the heavy woods, to nothing at all.

Mass for the Grace of a Happy Death

A bunch of us
always standing in doorways
down by the center of town
opposite the drugstore or
over by the Bowlaway with its
five lanes of candlepin—in
a city you might think a gang,
but not here in our little
blue village, tourists gone
for the season and us bumming
cigarettes from one another,
rain coming down in the dark,
somebody telling jokes, punching,
the usual stuff because nobody
wanted to sit at home like his
father or uncle or older brother,
stuck and humbled, no point
to much of anything, every
now and then a broken window or
some stolen hootch, sometimes
the solemn story repeated
from mouth to mouth on the same
gloomy steps, like a prophecy,
like when one of the boats went
down in December cold, all hands,
and we knew every one of them,
gave our versions, told our
reasons—too much weight
up on deck, out too far in
bad seas, greedy, too young
to be in the pilot house, bad
luck: Every one of us under
those drizzly eaves repeating
the mysteries until we were
satisfied, for a while, that

what finally rose from us was
the benediction unspoken—*not me,
not me, not me*—and waiting
awhile after that prayer finished
itself before we drifted off
along the sidewalks to our houses,
knowing that we'd stayed away
long enough, that the lights
would be out and everyone asleep.

II.

LAMENTATION

The awful thing is that beauty is mysterious as well as terrible. God and the devil are fighting there, and the battlefield is the heart of man. But a man always talks about his own ache.

—Fyodor Dostoyevsky
The Brothers Karamazov

Codeine

All those long, blank years
had to go by before we discovered Orpheus—
Orpheus! Imagine a life before him,
without him. It doesn't seem possible,
and yet it must have been: winter coat
of brown cotton, fur collar tucked up
around his ears, roaming the record stores,
hanging out down on Charles Street with
his pitiful guitar, G, C, D7th, F, a little
finger-picking, his eye on some empty sorrow
in a black skirt, always looking over his shoulder.
Don't think for a minute he didn't love
going down into the hot bone of his own limbs,
sinking into those subterranean visions
where the old boat croaked at its ratlines
and death had to squat in the mud,
abandoned on the wrong side of the river.
This has nothing to do with phony prescriptions
or getting some college kid to sign
for the medicine: this is about a song
that comes up from the underworld,
following Orpheus in his corduroy hat
when he rises, sick and shaking,
obsessed with some honeyed thing
he's left behind, and the memory
of one perfect voice singing,
calling him back for it.

Stealing

Dropped over the fence and rolled
to the side of the house, dark
for nights, the owners gone back
to wherever they go, the drama
of my own stealth so alien
to the world of real people
I wanted to laugh, even as I
slipped beneath the window, felt
its casing with the palm
of my glove, judged against it
and pressed along the shadows to
the cellar door, an inspiration,
cracked it open and crouched down
the steps, penlight on, scoping
the next move in the light's needle:
the second door, moldy, padlocked—
tore away the hasp with the pry-bar
and entered the web-hung cellar,
cold under the rough beams, found
the ladder and trapdoor and rose
hard to a small hallway, smoothing
back the heavy rug over the hatch,
in now, the bulky shapes of furniture
blooming in my night-vision as
I cupped the little light, let its
glow ooze from between my fingers:
Now the search, slow, comfortable,
easy, the town dead in sleep, nothing
to halt this trespass: empty
dresser, stripped bed, medicine
cabinet clean, worthless flatware
in the kitchen drawers, the television
too heavy to lug out of there
on a winter night, some records
I still remember, names

that I would only connect
after years: *Piaf, Vivaldi,*
and in the bookcase a photograph,
two naked men, one's face buried
between the thighs of the other,
something I moved from quickly
but came back to again before
I left with some small things
in my pockets, among them
a silk necktie and a deck of cards:
Then out the side door, nudging
it quietly locked behind,
bending past the brittle hedge
and heading toward the beach
where only the guilty might ever
see me slipping home, not thinking
that someday this might be
a memory I'd try to wake from
saying, *no, that could never
have been me, not me,* but walking
then in the quarter moon, an exuberant
wind on my face, celebrating
how I'd gone out again,
pushed my fingers into
some stranger's heart, and me
the only one to know.

Boston

Where we'd go down to the park
and huddle under the stone bridge,
smoking joints, nothing
in our heads, all living together
in a big place up near Brookline,
no heat, strangers blowing in
from New York or the Cape,
come to hang out, score, bring news,
have parties, hold seances,
stand around the kitchen range
and watch while someone cooked
dilaudid in a spoon. In November
we waited for the draft, one
dark-haired boy so distraught
and miserable he had a friend
jump from the hearth of our ruined
fireplace onto his cocked ankle,
a calculated, sure deferment:
but that violence shook the house,
the jumper horrified, the boy
amazed with pain and the sound
of whatever snapped in his body.
A heavy girl no one liked
held his head as he writhed—
he was high—we told him not
to do it high—and we brought
him down with seconal. Later,
six or seven of us sat around
in blankets on the floor,
and the girl said, "You know,
every one of us is going to go
to Hell when we die," still stroking
the boy's sweat-matted hair, his eyes
shining like nails in the bad light.
That was the night that someone

pried open the plastered flue
and burned a part of the banister,
and we watched the little fire
and told one another the simple losers'
lies about what we would do someday,
place and distance always building
some picture of desire: Mexico, California,
Montreal, the thickened nouns
leaving their saccharin on the tongue
as though we could walk down the stairs
and vanish along some privileged road
and not old Beacon Street, lit
by a chipped moon, where the battered trolleys
loaded up their fares and lurched
beneath a hail of sparks, rocked
and disappeared beneath the ground.

R and R

In Manila some men came
and locked a young girl, naked,
in a room with us, eight
or ten drunk marines and sailors
who had rotated back for a week of rest
and who had laid their good money down
and I can still remember the smell of her,
the tight black thatch under her belly,
the gold casing on her front tooth,
the way she laughed on each of our laps
just long enough to tease us before
she leapt to the next in the circle,
her skin like a soft glove over bones,
her bones like a separate animal
lying in wait under leaves.

Later someone bought her for the day.
The rest of us settled in other rooms,
into the boiled sheets and humidity
with the pretty girls in bright slips
who could not say our names, who
rode us like nightmares past the edges
of any desire, fierce, dark, rocking
creatures, working us like furies
then slipping off in the night
down streets forbidden to us, back
to lives we could neither reach nor imagine,
leaving us to lie alone in the damp beds,
trembling, sleepless, smoking cigarettes,
watching the slits in the wooden shutters,
waiting for morning, for some sign
of the calm and the light.

Mission

You don't really want to look, buttressed
as you are in your explosive seat,
but you turn and lean
and stare down at the shifting
darkness as the pilot's sure curve
sweeps a wave from your stomach,
and there, below, drives the pulpit of lights
as small as a stick in the wind:
the deck. You pass it and come about,
line up on approach, the planeguard destroyer
passing under you as it shadows
aft of the flattop, and then your body
falls into the tremendous *bang*
of the arresting wires, the hook
dragging you to a stop, snapping
your neck like a locker-room towel.
Can we do this—really? is what you ask
as you walk in your clumsy gear, now
in the vaulted nave of the hangar bays,
the men hustling at the planes
beneath the brash lights, everywhere
motion and clamor: *Yes, we can.*
We can fly in ways you wouldn't dream,
find ourselves in places that never existed
except for the stretch of our bitter will.
And you find that you want to do it
all again, every part of it, the hiss
and hurl of the catapult, and the breathless
dip into that swale of wind
as you clear the bow and power up,
and you want to swing out over
the night-blackened sea and rise
in the air to whatever they ask of you
until you are spent and terrified
and one more time bank to the edge
of prayer as you circle for the ship,
the iron mother, your violent home.

Lookouts, Foul Weather

We beat our way topside up ladders
and braced—my partner and I—
in a battened room under the masts
because our usual decks were awash
in flumes of water, black, indistinguishable
against the fields of other black, the earth
without its familiar hard facts—no stones,
roads, clods, trees, prairies—the sky
come down to heave under no star, to lock
us in an iron world that kept falling
from under our feet. The storm shuddered
our eighth of a mile of keel and twisted
the catwalks down to trash. We propped
our night-glasses against the view-slits
as though we really might see something,
as if any point of light auguring through
such layers of weather wouldn't show only
as a quick trace, just an ephemeral streak
to set us talking in our heads until
we thought it away, some ghost, some small
idea glimmering at the back of our cells,
winking its half-life and dying back.
There was no hope for anything outside
this banging skin. We rode for hours,
feet spread for balance, shoulders hunched
in canvas-and-fur jackets, smoking, nipping
a flask of Southern Comfort, feeling the weight
of each collapsing sea start to bury us,
feeling the long shiver each time we hammered back up,
every seam caught in some broken low note of chaos,
bulkheads shimmying and the ship rising
to a music of its own order, all that steel
come alive and each weld holding, singing.

South

What rivers are these? What
forests and fruits are these?

Crossed the Border
and came into desert,
drunk under stars, light
shivering in the spines
of the cholla and saguaro,
and we stopped the old car
by the dry tracks of a stream
so we could piss, crack
new quarts of warm Tecate
and drive again down
the latch of darkness
until morning and a shamble town,
sand streets, tumbleweeds
as big as heads bounding
past the shut doorways,
shared prickly pear and tortas
and mescal with the Indian girls
in the whorehouse there,
came down hard and slow,
sleeping under our Navy blankets
on the car's vinyl seats,
waking finally to the tough street-kids
pounding on the windshield and calling
us names as they begged for pesos,
their voices clipping the morning cold,
and we passed them beer, gave them
a handful of money, undershirts,
motor oil, cigarettes, cranked
the engine and pointed south again,
cottonmouthed, wanting only to drive,
still enough time then to never think
about turning back—drinking, throwing
our empties through the open windows,
watching the small carrion-birds flutter
like hands along the margins
of the broken-down road.

At Sea, Tonkin

Night always spread up from the horizon,
clouds rolling like something from the mind
and not of the world,
purple, orchid, plum, gigantic,
sweeping the last tongues of light
under their vast curves and arches,
and then in the quiet of the night-watches,
when only the distant pulse of the engines
hinted motion, the stars would quarry through
and the galaxy would bend
its broad spine over us.

Napping in a fuel station
or out on the wires—the catwalks—
sometimes you could sense the sea in a roll
and then you might half-dream some place of repose,
a bend in a creek lush with duckweed
or perhaps simply the beach
and a line of palms beyond.
At times it seemed almost possible
to empty yourself of all desire and responsibility,
as though you could find a way out of the body
and then a way to return, but not here to this.
There were times you'd almost gamble on it.

But then there was always a clank of chain,
shouts carrying over the lighted flattop,
a heeling to the wind, and you rose,
saw the relief crews
getting the jets ready,
and you left the air,
went below down ladders,
down the long columns of the red night-lights,
looking for another darkness.

Love is the Power Which Impels One to Seek the Beautiful

Ed came back without a leg. He lived in the dumpy little frame house next to the dumpy little frame house where Tom and I lived with Tom's girlfriend. Nights we'd hear him, crazy, screaming at his Irish setters. He was trying to paint things on stretched canvasses. Ed had been Navy, too, but Corpsman. Compared to him, Tom and I had had an easy life. We all understood things, though. We rode in my old Ford van out to the city college every morning and took classes on the GI Bill. It wasn't a lot of money. Ed got more because of his leg. We liked to sit around in Ed's place and smoke and drink whiskey. I read aloud from poems out of my Introduction to Literature book. Tom read Plato and Schopenhauer to us. He painted too, big gray canvasses with no people ever in them. One night one of the setters chewed up all of Ed's paintings. Ed raved all night and Tom's girlfriend had to take the dogs because she thought Ed would kill them. Ed had a false leg, but he never wore it. He kept it on a clotheshook on the wall. The VA used to give us Valium whenever we asked, big brown bottles of it. We all shared. Every month we got food stamps, and Tom's girlfriend bought us wine by the case. I believe we all loved one another. City colleges were free then in California. We did all right. Later, we drifted apart. We all wound up going to different universities. I don't know where Ed is anymore. I don't remember the last time I saw him. Tom is a minister now in a small town in the West. Now, after all these years of reading poems, I may finally understand certain questions of form. There is the line with its heartbeat, and there is language with its catalog of figures, and there is symmetry and breath. Every beginning demands an end, every curve a consummation, and the world and our lives must locate themselves in image or cease to exist. This could be a kind of *Longing* or a kind of *Will*. In seeking beauty it is sometimes necessary to reject a familiar or even an attractive form. If a symmetry is broken, we begin again. In some things failure is impossible.

Hitch

Heading for Berkeley, 1972,
hitched up Route 99,
the Central Valley, night
chill coming down the groves
as the last heat flickered
up from the blacktop, big
rigs blasting by, sucking
wind, diesel smoke bittering
the sky, and when the last
truck hit the airhorn and never
even slowed, we walked
the long hill up to a field
of cotton, crept among
the rows and laid ourselves down,
my belly to her back, the skinny
girl who had been my partner since
Bakersfield, those last
hundred miles, my hands clasped
over her small breasts,
our cover a wool rack-blanket
I had carried from the Navy
when I left. Once or twice
something sped by out on the road,
cowls of light opening in the air,
but we didn't move. The ground fog
puddled up around us dreaming
its way along the ditches, cold
as water seeping into our denim,
and we dozed, the slightest
motion from either of us
making a pocket where the chill
wedged in, and we clung through
fitful sleep to keep it out.
I woke later in the false dawn,
heard the low rumbling in the earth,
understood that human voices carried
through the boles of mist and then saw

the yellow headlights of the truck
crawling the ditchline, a flatbed
loaded with *braceros* coming into
the field. The girl sat up
suddenly and we watched them pass,
one man seeing us, whistling
shrilly through his fingers
and waving a quick sharp wave,
a warning, *Get out of here,*
and we let them go by and crept
up to the road, still joined
by the blanket, shivering,
banging each other at the shoulders
until we huddled again at the roadside,
gray light now rising in the valley,
a motor climbing the long crease
of highway, somewhere still beyond sight,
and we let that hope rise, too,
that this was it, the ride out,
and when we laughed it seemed
for no reason, but I remember
what it felt like then, believing
that something brilliant waited
just beyond whatever it was that cradled
our skins, and that we moved to it
every time we moved at all, simply
because we could. And when the semi
wheeled by, hauling a mountain of
gnarled sugar beets, and the driver
stabbed his thumb over his shoulder
back down the hill and kept on going,
we only laughed again, sat
on the road's edge, lit cigarettes
and cupped our fingers around the tips,
breathed the smoke deep and waited.

What Death With Love Must Have To Do

Summer night, window open,
muggy breeze coming off the water,
and somebody's at it, really getting
hammered, the *oh,oh,oh,oh,oh,* sailing
on the air, the most miserable
sound in the world when you're alone
and understand that something
in your nature is twisted so
you'll never be exactly convinced
by that sort of rapture—too mindless,
too disconnected from the great
redeeming sorrows of the world
that make a heart want to batter
its own hollow into another heart,
not sex now, but something else,
something you've come to suspect
is a lie: listen, there she goes again,
irrepressible, you can taste the sweat
on the honeysuckle, you can measure
the cadence in your own pulse: all
joy locked in the body? All flight
subsumed in this? It's said that
every action, every thought uses up
something commensurate somewhere else
so that the vast world of stars and particles
is diminished, brought closer to chaos
by every living choice: how do we settle
with that knowledge? How do we sleep,
after, spent, tingling in every cell
because we have been loved, knowing
that somewhere the darkness has advanced,
knowing that we will wake again craving
the rampant touch, the inflamed kiss.

Lamentation

Someone has come
    and whacked through the brush

    on the side of the hill, and now
a long yellow surveyor's thread
    stretches down the swath
that could only have been bulldozed,

    so clean and complete are its lines,
so explicit the white lacerations
      on the wrist-thick branches that have been piled
        into a thatched wall,

      and I walk this odd fissure
    along the property line
      ignored for decades, now an easement,
        soon a road:
            It is spring
in the fourth year of the drought. Even so,
    the year's scant rain on the pastures
has brought up a green silkening

      that stretches away to the farthest fences
and the bright green hooks of the wild cucumber
    churn along the shining oak,
      and ceanthus bristles, impudent

among the manzanita, the manzanita itself
    blooming in delicate puckers
      where the bees suck and roll,
    starbursts that will soon dry and vanish:
        Higher,
from this hill's flank the quitclaim covenants
    of a hundred years show like patchwork
on the valley's soil—fence-lines

and firebreaks, the avocado groves, oranges,
the wild oaks, the alfalfa,

and lately
the great bruises of the new houses that come
in clusters, that bring work and money,
that advance from the west, pawn
and bishop, thigh by thigh, to gild
the sunlight with their ochre roofs.

In the oldest stories
God gave up the world as a rod
according to which we might perfect ourselves
and move from his silence into his light
even as the barbed wire moves to rust
and the fence-posts wither, and the mushrooms
send up their last white prayer
from the nave of the ruined log,

but there is no palate here anymore
for the old dialectics of order and chaos:
nothing has prepared us for this harrowing
when the last coyote hangs his tooth
in the poisoned bait,
and the bats diminish to tales
in the holy books,
and the owl flies
to the false lights of the north, and the beetle
and the tarantula dance
in the ravenous sugars of malathion:
And so in this strange year of the early heat
the hills prepare to receive their multitudes
and I climb again, crawling at times, pulling
on the shin-bones of scrub trees
until the tin roofs of our own outbuildings

show themselves
through the tent of the eucalyptus

all the way down to the pig-iron
of the dead tractor and the mouth in the earth
where the pump-engine
whines for ground water,

and there in the bright polygon of irrigated grass
and the cluster of apple and peach trees
my wife and her mother
have gone out with a bowl
and from this distance they seem to be gathering
blossoms—

blossoms, the women's shadows
darkening the grass like two long others
moving among them as they reach
their arms into the trees:

It is impossible to catch their words now, tinkling
like the wind-chime, that reach me
only in scattered bits, the voices
tumbled and dissembled,
not easy to tell
what they have walked out to claim
in a season that will bring no fruit.

III.
PSALM

Pleni sunt coeli et terra gloria tua.

— from the Sanctus

Psalm

Walked among the oldest paths
in that easy wood of pine and larch
to the side of a hill and the faces
of the old tombs, sod-roofed
and iron-doored, and thought this
would be like the cave, the skull-
place where the soldier slept
and the stone was rolled and the body's
absence revealed, the stories already
walking the roads under the massive
oaks—the wounds, the tongues of fire,
the broken bread in the mouth becoming more,
and then more.
              And so what if it is only
what they've come to call text, this language
of names that might not even be names,
for where are Mark's bones, or the cisterns
of Luke's house, and where did the word John
squat at the cook-fires turning a small
bird on a spit?
              And when the scattered friends
were once gathered, can we believe exactly
that his flesh was unrecognizable to them,
and if so, what lake was it where he commanded
the fishes to fill the nets, and which one
of them counted the numbers of the catch,
and is one hundred and fifty-three the same
now as it was then, or has that figure's
significance changed also, in the manner
of miracles, which have effaced themselves
into reenactment, blood into wine, force
into ritual, a world made too small
for all the books yet to be written?
              And the bodies
here under the mud hills have moldered down

to absence, the families named on the rusty
grates have vanished from all the rosters,
most certainly girded and carried by others
where they did not wish to go, and howsoever
they suffered they lay quietly on the third day
and each day thereafter, never led out
even as far as Bethany, though yet there are
two I can still remember, one white and wild-
haired and the other in a seaman's cap,
                                        stepping
out into the coldest time, a winter when
all the boards in the yard were frozen
and this wet earth numbered fewer graves,
and the black limbs of the apple tree
lay streaked with a scant new snow,
and breath trumpeted from mouth and nostril,
and these two hard men with no use for rest,
Great Uncle and Grandfather, carried small
coal shovels and galvanized buckets,
walking silently as they strewed ashes
over the icy pavings between house and shed,
and a small face watched through an empty window,
wishing then they might turn and admonish
to follow them, and learning soon enough
that every promise is to be fulfilled,
                                and if remembering them
I say, *stay with us, for it is toward evening
and the day is far from spent*, it will not matter,
for a spirit has not flesh and bones,
and the dead are not mindful of our intentions,
and it is not by signs or figures
or their manipulation, but only by another's breath
that these dead are raised for the small moment
to walk so tenuously among the tenuous living.

Hymn

Then sing about appetite, that lovely first
green serpent of a thought, bringing with it
its trace of the Tree of the Knowledge
of Good and Evil, whereby, we are told,

the first mother and father tumbled
into the complicated well of death.
Perhaps it's a matter of too much order
tilting the perfect dogwood and lilac

to hang heavily over the footpaths
that leach the garden in the second version
in the old book, where God roams
among the swinging figs and spiders' silks,

a presence as clear as yours or mine, for
*the man and the woman heard the sound
of the Lord God walking in the cool of day,*
and now what we ponder is the absence

of that Father of fathers, the vanishing
of that literal earth of first naming
where the man took into his mouth the various
shapes of the humid air, and from him

flew the wedges of the world—*iron, delight,
whistle, bat, finger, thigh,* each word
prying its difference from the others,
until every wistful corner bloomed

in the original, baffling profusion of *things*.
Name what you want: *Heart, beauty,*
wholeness, salvation, the sound of the Father
walking the shimmering lavish growth

into existence around him. Something
is never there, and we wish and wish,
stars, fontanel, apple, gorging the world
with nothing but tongue and desire.

The Wine at Cana

Snow. And then more snow. All
night the night fell around us
as the drifts rode like sea-swells
against the house and hedge
and we began to sink into the sleep
of storm, a troubling comfort
where things did not keep their
practical and familiar shine.
For hours we burned the kerosene lamp
against the quit electric light,
and the coal in the black hod
dwindled and the wind skirled
down the chimney's brick. My
mother's face hung like a moon
by lamplight, pale, with all the gold
of her eyeglasses gleaming, working
away at something that has long withered
and disappeared—and my stepfather
lost in the mire of his angers,
breathing through his teeth, fiddling
some small device that has likewise
failed and vanished, though a palm of wax
sits clearly on the table with
a wooden darning egg and a glass
bowl filled with cigarette ash.
Who could imagine these two as lovers,
sitting among the cloistered ruins
of their love, and who might imagine
a knock on the door in such a night,
a guest come to sit and keep watch
with them while the storm sailed
and to drink a bit of something
warmed in glass by the coalfire,
something plain and hopeful as any

hope of yours, brought to a new luster,
that dull and puzzling bitterness
that had come from beyond them and settled
so frighteningly within the cached
green bottles suddenly lifted, and for
this moment a lightness, a blessing.

Offering

From one hill you can sight along
the marble headstones, a shoulder
in the earth where the land
sweetens down a long curve
and ice gnaws at the light
nesting in the sharp husks
of grass and thistle: Who
among them once lived upright
and loved her neighbor, took
in the despised, sheltered
the unloved, boiled linens
in a copper tub during the time
of the influenza, swabbed
the wracked bodies of the sick?
Or who leaned over the lime-
washed fence and plucked
unseen the crabbed apples
from his neighbor's tree, spit
on the planks of the walk
and told stories of his time
on the water, the gale that almost
washed him from the mast,
then biting the hard fruit,
laughing, ticking a space
between his teeth, thinking
of the woman he loved once
in some far place where
there was no hope of anything
everlasting, remembering
only the way a certain light
shivered from her lips when she
smiled, when she leaned
on his young arm, still hard
as a board, and it pleased
her that he had tasted words
on what was for him
her strange dark tongue.

By What Steps the Divine Madnesses Raise the Soul

She told me her breasts ached
and slid my hands up and over them
there in the front seat of her mother's car,
my mouth raw from kissing and her own
mouth so wet and hard against mine
that in all that rapt confusion of breath
and tongue I had no sense of where
we were going, as though, then,
everything led someplace, making
each other come with just our
fingers, over and over, until
we hurt from it, and the windshield
glazed over with our steam and our smells:
Beyond us, in our own private place,
the winter woods buckled down a black lane,
and we stepped outside, dizzy, into the slap
of air, holding by the hand and shaking
until the sky steadied above us, big
Orion lumbering through the bare limbs,
something I could name for her before
we climbed back in, shivering with cold now
and loving for the first time something we
couldn't identify yet—not each other,
certainly not ourselves—but a beginning
in the deep shadows as we backed down
the lane, keeping the car darkened until
we felt the road's shoulder and then
headed in those bright immortal bodies
toward the waiting lights of town.

Plain Song

And so it comes to exile, as I always
knew it would, all this fair shape
exhaling into brittleness and dysfunction,
the singing that I thralled my life to
having become nothing less than
the tinny running of the salt creek,
the sound of freezing water
creeping through the teeth of freezing stones:
Here I took up the old boat, deaf
by my own will to anything but this savage calling,
and pushed that weathered bow into the broad stream
and poled and skulled up the blue runs
where the tide weaves swift among
the straw loaves and grassy shoulders,
where a single heron rose on drumming wings
and pipers tumbled in shallows, and the ragged tomcods,
so late in season, still marshalled their numbers
in the brooding riffs; came then to the island
as if bent by an old canting, ineluctable,
the chaotic land gull-trashed and purple
with its rife nettle and briar, and beached
that bone skiff and scuttled inward along
the deer trails and rabbit runs that snaked
the clumped, cold sanctuary at the center, spreading
with stung hands the switches and collars of bramble,
wearied and driven toward that uncompromising heart.

Curandera

She burned curled leaves in a bowl.
She walked from Guatemala to do this.
She buried dead for a thousand
miles and planted her own teeth
in nests and furrows along the way.
Her doors alone were clean of the glyphs
and gang-sign that razed the long boulevard.
Last week she healed a wound, and once
she dried up a woman's sex to ruin a husband.
Her breath was sharp with fish. She
asked fifteen dollars and took my hand
in hers, felt at the bones beneath
the skin. She could have taken a knife
and flayed me and nothing in her eyes
would have changed. I asked her questions
about luck and the love of a particular
woman. Votive candles burned behind her head.
On a poster the Sacred Heart of Jesus
wept blood. She had wrapped Rosaries
around her wrist, the way my old aunt
once did. Motors came and went in the street.
When she finally spoke to me, she said
"You are too proud." I wasn't sure
I heard her correctly. "Pride! Pride!"
she said then in English. "What more?" I asked.
She smiled. "There is a skull under your face."
"And under yours, too," I said. She
liked this. She squeezed my hand and rocked
back in her chair and laughed. *"Now*
you are ready to understand me," she said.

Mexican Woman, Hair in Braids,
Caught In Barbed Wire on the Side of I-5

Five, maybe six cars—a major bust
at the INS roadblock, the dark young
boys, eight or ten of them, running
crazy for the beach, cutting in front
of our car and weaving across
eight lanes of traffic. On the right-
hand shoulder a *coyote* hustling riders
out of his white Pontiac, panic
everywhere, the men and women dressed
in odd cuts and colors, something
very wrong, everyone too obvious,
and a middle-aged man bending,
spreading the strands of the barbed
wire that fenced the shoulder
from a sloping field of dead grass.
But the woman does not crawl
in the proper latitudes, the spikes
on the wire hike her rough dress
above her heavy thighs, her braids
swing black when she turns and looks
at the puckered snags—waist, hem,
bodice—a wail of defeat as a dust-
devil spins behind the government truck
tearing up the dirt firebreak, and then
her hand settling as though forming
a sign, fingers carefully poised
and gently plucking at the wire.

Where Do You Sleep?

I warn my son against eating the red berries
on the chaparral hillside—coyote food lumping
the odd scats we see on the clay road
that edges the long pasture
where the wild geese come down at twilight
to gabble like the crowds at the town fair,
strangers' voices winnowed through the limbs
of the bordering oaks. Once we saw
a bobcat, like a pistol-shot on the haunches
of a jackrabbit diving into the expedient dusk,
and then darkness came, and my wife's mother
walked out from the screened porch,
her breath a mist in cold starlight,
her eyes on the deepening hills.
"No fires tonight," is all she said
and nipped her bourbon, and it was true
we saw no lights then under the black
angle of ridge where the big cat had vanished,
no suspected camps of the *illegals* who make
their way up this secluded valley, pushing north,
who walk up to our sagging, whitewashed house
to barter work for sandwiches, dollars,
a chance to wash their children
in the spray of the black hose
coiled on the side of the cow-barn.

And on our rummage sometimes
through the oak knees and barbed wire, along
the steep rills of the dung-lined creek,
I look for *tramp-signs*—the cross of sticks
or diamond of stones that mark a house simply, *yes* or *no*.
We are far enough from the border
to only hear of its drama, the *other* coyotes,
their craft of promise, the government dogs

rooting spoor in the waste of the dry arroyos,
but we may be marked by some emblem here
for they come, the men and the boys mostly, lean as rails
and I squat in the dirt of the dooryard with them,
my once-good Spanish rusting like the fence wire
or the rabbit cages stacked in the tall weeds and bamboo:
Here is some money for food. The Senora wants
the weeds knocked down in the old pasture
and will pay you the rest when you finish.
She doesn't need the work done. When the family
comes on weekends, her sisters chide, *It's dangerous.*
You don't know what they might do.
She never argues, but she never stops hiring them,
learns their names, speaks to them in signs
and single words, tries to learn
where they sleep, where they come from,
and where they think they are going.

Our valley within the valley: I have
never felt the wind here, but nights
the cold air flows down the cleft
like a slow river, invisible
under the lip of the low ridges, touching to life
each leaf and branch, brimming up to glaze the moon
and even the stars as they wheel their long track
around the pole. An owl flies, bats rise
like scraps from a fire, and something sets
our own dogs barking in the brush behind the sheds.
I rise, too, and softly walk inside to where my son
breathes heavily in his sleeping bag
adorned with bright monsters. He shudders
at my footfall, tosses in some deep dream,
and I lay a hand to his forehead, brush back
his hair and spend a minute in his clean boy-smell

before I go back outdoors. The dogs
have run off, and the sky
has become its own river of light.
I sit perfectly still. I cannot
tell if the owl has settled
somewhere beyond the pastures and I hear
the long night-rhythms of its call,
or if I hear the slow persistent lilt
of a single human voice
sifting down, out of the hills.

Sand

Beyond the sagging porches bleached
of paint and caulking, up the lanes
where the last spiny beach-grass
strops itself on the weather,
the dunes are tumbling toward us,
sliding like surf under their own
plush curves, snuffing the scraggly
pine and alder, creeping year by year
so that bulldozers are stationed
out on Route Six, where the town narrows
to a wrist, and men in deep gloves
push back, push back. It's useless.
Even the red-slatted snow fences
eventually go under, don't even form
the slightest drift, for this is silica
not weather: this coming forward
bears the weight of stone. Once
we went through woods to the very bourne
where the sandhills licked the tops
of the crabbed, smothered trees,
and we sat and listened, as if we might
hear a movement like the soft running
of grains in a narrowed glass. The moon
swelled, and a chill coughed out of the bracken.
Seaward, the dunes rose and we climbed them,
up out of vegetable tangles and into
the unbroken mineral shine, luminous
everywhere, eyes aching for all that sameness,
our oracle of rigid sleep under the pale drudge
that would continue no matter what we did,
taking everything down in its way, even
while its shoulders lifted in their vacant shrug
toward that other, larger, distant light.

Some Kind of Blues

Harp, they say, as for angel,
or bone sliding down the neck
of the ax, bourbon swilling
in delirious tears all over
the linoleum: it's true for just
this moment that you'll never
have to die, true that love
smells good in a long dress and
will last forever except for
the mistake one of you will make,
so consider these harsh notes
decaying like one of those
desperate kisses that don't
ever get off the bus, the woman
saying to you with her eyes
oh, I know just where you ache,
and the second guitar, Jesus,
suddenly *he's* taking it away,
all those chords adding up
to something that shouldn't
have surprised you, but it does:
it surprises you. It makes
you want to weep, and you've been
through all *that* before, and
so you move your feet and nod
your head. You don't even
have to look around—they're
all nodding their heads too.
Yes, everyone is saying,
Yes, yes, yes.

Eucharist

Kneeling at the altar rail,
head back, and the priest and his angels
sliding toward each dry mouth,
gold pyx and incantation
in the rich Latin, air swelling
with unmistakable, absolute presence
so that the walk back to the pew
with the Host fusing to the tongue
was a drunken float, an abeyance
of the small laws of the body,
everything shining in complete
relevance and perspective, the men
stiff and solemn in their awkward clothes,
and the women's faces shining behind
their Sunday veils, the girls
sleepy and bored, and even then
the holiness of their sex lying like
the scent of blossoms in their curved laps
while everything reached to become something else,
some transfigured perfection that had been pledged
to us and that we tried to carry into
the uncertain world when the Mass had ended,
walking down the broad steps among
the gleaming heads and starched hems,
the flat musty taste dissolving,
and the brazen light of morning arcing,
aching under our hungry eyes.

Notes

1. The Mass for the Grace of a Happy Death is a specific Mass of supplication, taken from the old Catholic Missal.

2. The epigraph to the first section is taken from *Silex Scintillans* by Henry Vaughan.

3. "Christ in the World of Matter": Title is taken from *Hymn of the Universe* by Teilhard de Chardin.

4. "South": Epigraph is taken from Whitman's *Leaves of Grass*.

5. "Love is the Power Which Impels One to Seek the Beautiful": Title is taken from *Commentary On Plato's Symposium* by Marsilio Ficino.

6. "What Death With Love Should Have to Do": Title is taken from the poem "A Hymn to the Name and Honor of the Admirable Saint Teresa" by Richard Crashaw.

7. "By What Steps the Divine Madnesses Raise the Soul": Title is taken from *Commentary On Plato's Symposium* by Marsilio Ficino.

About the Author

Frank X. Gaspar was born and raised in Provincetown, Massachusetts and now lives in Southern California where he teaches at Long Beach City College. He served in the Navy during the Vietnam Conflict, and after his discharge he earned an MFA from the University of California, Irvine. He's published poems and short stories in numerous journals, including *The Nation, The Kenyon Review, The New England Review, The Georgia Review* and others. His first collection of poems, *The Holyoke*, won the Morse Prize in 1988. He's been an NEA Fellow, a John Atherton Fellow at Breadloaf and a Walter Dakin Fellow at Sewanee (University of the South).

Anhinga Prize For Poetry

Selection: **Judge:**

Frank X. Gaspar   1994
Mass for the Grace of a Happy Death   Joy Harjo

Janet Holmes   1993
The Physicist at the Mall   Joy Harjo

Earl S. Braggs   1992
Hat Dancer Blue   Marvin Bell

Jean Monahan   1991
Hands   Donald Hall

Nick Bozanic   1989
The Long Drive Home   Judith Hemschemeyer

Julianne Seeman   1988
Enough Light to See   Charles Wright

Will Wells   1987
Conversing with the Light   Henry Taylor

Robert Levy   1986
The Whistle Maker   Robin Skelton

Judith Kitchen   1985
Perennials   Hayden Carruth

Sherry Rind   1984
The Hawk in the Backyard   Louis Simpson

Ricardo Pau-Llosa   1983
Sorting Metaphors   William Stafford

Other Books From Anhinga Press

P.V. LeForge — *The Secret Life of Moles*

Gary Corseri — *Random Descent*

Michael Mott — *Counting the Grasses*

Yvonne Sapia — *The Fertile Crescent*

Rick Lott — *Digging for Shark Teeth*

Ryals and Decker, eds. — *North of Wakulla: An Anhinga Anthology*

Jordan and Shows, eds. — *Cafe at St. Marks: The Apalachee Poets*

Van Brock, ed. — *A Spot of Purple is Deaf*

DATE DUE

APR '02